KU-523-370

34 4124 0014 5986

SPECIAL EDITION
Happy Birthday, ROMAN TRIBUNE
300 years old today!

ROMAN TRIBUNE

11th June AD 343

Andrew Langley

raintree

a Capstone company — publishers for children

Raintree is an imprint of Capstone Global Library Limited, a company incorporated in England and Wales having its registered office at 264 Banbury Road, Oxford, OX2 7DY – Registered company number: 6695582

www.raintree.co.uk
myorders@raintree.co.uk

Text © Capstone Global Library Limited 2018
The moral rights of the proprietor have been asserted.

All rights reserved. No part of this publication may be reproduced in any form or by any means (including photocopying or storing it in any medium by electronic means and whether or not transiently or incidentally to some other use of this publication) without the written permission of the copyright owner, except in accordance with the provisions of the Copyright, Designs and Patents Act 1988 or under the terms of a licence issued by the Copyright Licensing Agency, Saffron House, 6–10 Kirby Street, London EC1N 8TS (www. cla.co.uk). Applications for the copyright owner's written permission should be addressed to the publisher.

Edited by Helen Cox Cannons
Designed by Philippa Jenkins and Cynthia Della-Rovere
Original illustrations © Capstone Global Library Limited 2018
Picture research by Tracy Cummins
Production by Kathy McColley
Originated by Capstone Global Library Limited
Printed and bound in India

ISBN 978 1 4747 5476 7
22 21 20 19 18
10 9 8 7 6 5 4 3 2 1

British Library Cataloguing in Publication Data
A full catalogue record for this book is available from the British Library.

Acknowledgements
We would like to thank the following for permission to reproduce photographs: Alamy: ART Collection, 19 Middle, Heritage Image Partnership Ltd, 5 Top, INTERFOTO, 18 Middle Left, Kevin Britland, 23 Bottom; Capstone: 21 Top, Helen Cox Cannons, 9, Philippa Jenkins, 15, 29, Trevor Hughes, 4 Top, 6 (soldiers), Cover Middle, Cover Top; Dreamstime: Phillip Toddington, 22 Bottom, Stefano Venturi, 24 Left; Getty Images: Allison Leach, Cover Top Right, Eric VANDEVILLE/Gamma-Rapho, 4 Middle, M Dixon/ Print Collector, 26 Right; iStockphoto: hsvrs, 4 Bottom, PaulaConnelly, 22 Top, Roberto A Sanchez, 5 Bottom, uplifted, 14; Museum of London: 23 Top; Shutterstock: alessandro guerriero, 18 Top, Alexandr Zadiraka, 17 Top, antb, 19 Bottom, Binh Thanh Bui, 24 (turnip), bonchan, 24 (leek), Bukhta Yurii, 11 Right, coxy58, 27, Elina-Lava, 7, Emily Marie Wilson, 19 Top Left, Ernst Prettenthaler, 14 (sky), ESB Professional, 17 (wood), iconer, Cover (building icon), ieronim777, 8 (Mars), KKulikov, 17 (man), klenger, 27 Background, Kozlik, 16, Cover Bottom Right, luigi nifosi, Cover Middle Right, Matias DelCarmine, 8 (Minerva, Jupiter, Apollo), McCarthy's PhotoWorks, 6 (emperor), Michael Rosskothen, 10, 20, 21 Bottom, monticello, 24 (cabbage), motorolka, 24 (rosemary), Mr.prasong, Back Cover Design Element, Nattapon Spasuwonnakul, 17 Right (chicken), Nik Keevil, 28 Top Left, Only Fabrizio, 28 Right, oriori, 24 (walnut), Pooh photo, Cover (sky), Richard Peterson, 6 (elephant), shoot4pleasure, 28 Middle, Simon Annable, 21 Middle, spline_x, 24 (thyme), Stephane Bidouze, 17 Left (chicken), symbiot, 13 Left, Tomasz Szymanski, 1, Vitaly Korovin, Design Element, zcw, 24 (chestnuts); SuperStock: hwo/imageBROKER, 12, DeAgostini, 28 Bottom Left, Riccardo Sala/age fotostock, 18 Middle Right; © The Trustees of the British Museum: 18 Bottom; Thinkstock: Photos.com, 26 Left; Wikimedia: Museo de historia de Valencia, 25, Nilfanion, 11 Left, WellCome Images, 13 Right.

We would like to thank Dr Stephen Bowman at the University of the Highlands and Islands for his invaluable help in the preparation of this book.

Every effort has been made to contact copyright holders of material reproduced in this book. Any omissions will be rectified in subsequent printings if notice is given to the publisher.

All the internet addresses (URLs) given in this book were valid at the time of going to press. However, due to the dynamic nature of the internet, some addresses may have changed, or sites may have changed or ceased to exist since publication. While the author and publisher regret any inconvenience this may cause readers, no responsibility for any such changes can be accepted by either the author or the publisher.

INSIDE...

Happy birthday to us! 4

No deal 5

We're in charge now 6

London's burning 7

Religious news 8

Business news 10

Farming news 12

A day in the life 14

Letters to the editor 15

Celeb news 16

Fashion highlights 18

Handy hints 19

Travel news 20

Homes for sale 22

Food and drink 24

Arts and entertainment 26

For sale 28

Timeline 29

Glossary 30

Find out more 31

Index 32

Some words are shown in bold, **like this**. You can find out what they mean by looking in the glossary.

read on...

HAPPY BIRTHDAY TO US!

Editor Rufina Redtop writes:

Salve! (That's Latin for "Hello!") Welcome to this special birthday edition of the *Roman Tribune*. We're 300 years old this year!

It all began in AD 43, when the Emperor Claudius and his Roman troops invaded Britain and stayed here. There were bloody battles, but in the end we took charge and it became part of the Roman Empire. Since then, the Romans have brought huge changes to this island – paved roads and new towns, sewers and running water, better laws and lots of Latin words. Without us, Britons might never have had cats, calendars, cabbages or carrots. Imagine that!

To celebrate our 300th birthday, we've put together a selection of our favourite news stories from over the years. They are organized by subject, and you can find their dates beside each article. We hope you enjoy this look back at the past. Who knows what will happen next?

VESPASIAN VILLAS
Sales / Lettings

Stunning villas at bargain prices in Colchester, London, Bath, Chester, York and more. See our bargains of the week (right) before someone else snaps them up!

NO DEAL

British invasion attempt ends in failure

Kent, 55 BC

Well, we tried. Julius Caesar and our Roman troops recently landed in Britain for the very first time. His warships crossed the **Channel** from **Gaul** and reached Deal on the south coast. Fierce British warriors watched them from the cliffs as they arrived.

Our brave **legionaries** jumped down onto the beach. They charged at the Britons, who all ran away. But then Caesar's luck ran out. A big storm blew up and smashed most of our ships. Winter was coming and the food was running out. So Caesar decided to go back to Rome, vowing to return next year.

TOTAL RE-GAUL

Kent, 54 BC

Julius Caesar has been and gone – again. He landed in Britain with an even bigger army than before, getting as far as the River Thames. But this second invasion didn't last much longer than the first. A spokesman for Caesar said, "He was forced to go back to Gaul to put down a rebellion." But where does this leave our plans for Britain?

WE'RE IN CHARGE NOW
Claudius the Conqueror

Colchester, AD 43

The Romans have done it at last. Under the Emperor Claudius, we have invaded Britain and seized control. Even the great Julius Caesar couldn't do that! Britain is now firmly part of the Roman Empire.

Claudius didn't actually do much of the fighting. He left that to his tough old general, Aulus Plautius. Aulus landed with his army on the south coast. They chased the Britons inland and across the River Thames then forced them to surrender. Only then did Claudius arrive on the scene. He brought more soldiers and even some elephants! He led his forces on a triumphant march into the grand new city of Colchester to celebrate the great victory. But he didn't stay long. He'll soon be back in Rome – for another victory parade.

LONDON'S BURNING

Rebels on the rampage

London, AD 60

Roman rule is in danger. Queen Boudicca and her British **Iceni tribe**, plus other tribes, have raised a savage **revolt** and have shattered the Emperor's hold on Britain. They have murdered hundreds of Roman citizens here in the south-east of England.

Inspired by Boudicca, the Iceni destroyed the town of Colchester. When a Roman army was sent to defeat them, they smashed it as well. Now Boudicca has marched to London and set it on fire.

Why did she start this bloodbath? Well, for a start, on the death of her husband we stole the tribe's land and treasure. And some Roman soldiers beat Boudicca and attacked her daughters.

BOUDICCA BEATEN

Watling Street, AD 60

Panic over. A large Roman army under Suetonius Paullinus has crushed the Iceni rebels. The slaughter was terrible. Some people say that over 80,000 Britons died, including Boudicca herself. Roman Britain is safe again.

RELIGIOUS NEWS

PICK YOUR OWN GOD

AD 100

What do you believe in? Is it the Roman gods worshipped back in Rome, or the local gods worshipped here in Britain?

No problem! We Romans are pretty relaxed about it. You can follow any religion you want (as long as it doesn't include weird human sacrifice carried out

by those nasty **Druids**). In fact, some Roman and British gods are now being worshipped together. Here are some of the big pairings.

ROMAN		BRITISH
Minerva, goddess of wisdom	AND	**Sulis,** water goddess (in Somerset)
Mars, god of war	AND	**Cocidius,** god of hunting (in Cumbria)
Jupiter, god of sky and thunder	AND	**Toutatis,** god of the sky (in Lincolnshire)
Apollo, god of healing	AND	**Cunomaglos,** the dog prince (in Wiltshire)

RELIGIOUS NEWS

PUT TO DEATH
Beheaded for being a Christian

Hertfordshire, AD 250

By our religious affairs reporter, Percy Cutor

Gone are the days – not so long ago – when Britons could worship whatever god they liked. Nowadays it's especially dangerous to be a Christian. We Romans have to make sure that everyone respects our gods and our Emperor. And that sometimes means killing people who follow the faith of Jesus Christ.

The latest victim is a Roman man called Alban, from Verulamium. Locals in the town claim that he gave shelter to a Christian priest.

When soldiers arrived, Alban said he was the Christian priest. So they arrested him instead (while the real priest escaped).

Alban has been put to death. He was beheaded and buried nearby.

EMPEROR BACKS CHRISTIANITY

Rome, AD 312

In a sensational move, the Roman Emperor Constantine has given a thumbs-up to Christianity. About time! This comes years after the religion first became popular in Britain. Constantine has declared that, from now on, Christians can worship freely. It's too late for poor old Alban, though. He ought to be remembered in some way. Perhaps they'll name a town after him.

BUSINESS NEWS

DOORWAY TO EUROPE AND THE WORLD

London, AD 200

Wine from Gaul, olive oil from Spain, pottery from Greece, **amber** from the **Baltic**, spices from India, silk from China – these are just a few of the wonderful things you can find in London today.

London is Britain's biggest trading centre, thanks to the Romans. Goods flow in from all over the Empire and beyond. Ships sail up the River Thames and unload their amazing **cargo** at the docks.

The city has had its bad times. It's been burned down twice, in AD 60 and AD 130. But now it's been rebuilt into a very grand place. There's a huge **amphitheatre** for sport, a town hall, lots of public baths and an open **forum** where people can meet and go shopping. The whole thing is surrounded by a 6 metre (19 feet) high stone wall to keep out any baddies who rebel against us.

BUSINESS NEWS

MINE ALL MINE
Digging for Welsh gold

Dolaucothis, Dyfed, AD 110

Whoosh! With a roar, the water rushes out of the big tank. It races down the hillside, washing away soil and plants. Now I can see the rock underneath.

"That's where the gold is,"

says mine manager, Maximus Minus.

"Now all we have to do is dig it out."

A gang of slaves starts hacking away at the wet rock with hammers and picks. It's hard work, but they soon break off big chunks.

This is one way of mining gold at Dolaucothi, Britain's biggest Roman gold mine. They also dig rocks out of tunnels underground. But how do they extract the gold from the rock? "We grind up the chunks," says Max. "Then we heat them all up over a big fire. The gold in the rock melts and runs out. Simple!"

MONEY MAKER

London, AD 287

At last. Roman coins are being made in Britain – more than 200 years since we took over. The Roman leader Carausius has opened the first-ever official Roman **mint** in London. Now we'll never be short of cash.

FARMING NEWS

FARM OR PALACE?

By our farming correspondent Decimus Dungheap

Gloucestershire, AD 376

It's the poshest farm you've ever seen. Chedworth villa boasts **mosaic** floors, marble carvings, a grand bathhouse and a **temple**. It's even got a **shrine** to a water **nymph**. It's not a place for muddy boots!

And yet Chedworth is also a working farm, just like other Roman villas. There are hundreds of them all across southern Britain. Wheat and barley grow in the fields. Cattle and sheep chew on the grass. Pigs root around in the orchards. There are barns, dairies, stables and even blacksmiths' **forges**.

Two centuries ago, Chedworth was just a simple farmhouse with land. But over the last few decades, the owners have lavished pots of money on new buildings and luxury features here. They are obviously very rich and very powerful. Now it's more like a palace.

FARMING NEWS

YOU ARE WHAT YOU WHEAT

Storing enough grain

Dorset, AD 200

There are thousands of Roman soldiers and settlers in Britain. How on earth do we keep them well fed? Our most important food is wheat – lots of it – grown by Britain's farmers. And it's not just any old wheat. It's called spelt wheat. Our soldiers like spelt better than the native varieties of wheat.

There's one problem. The grain has to be stored through the long winters. But it has to be completely dry or it goes mouldy. So, after it is harvested, the wheat is put into a special dryer.

This is a narrow tunnel. At one end of the tunnel is a fire. At the other is a chimney called a flue, which draws the hot air from the fire along the tunnel. After a few hours, the grain is dry as a bone.

SHEAR MAGIC

Shepherds – don't take all day clipping those sheep. Get that fleece off in seconds with our new Roman **shears**. Solid iron and sharp as a razor. All the way from Italy.

Available from
Ivor Lamb,
XIV Sheep Street,
Baaaath

A DAY IN THE LIFE

This week...
ON THE WINDY WALL

Northumberland, AD 137

""Eee, it's chilly up here!"

says Geordius Maximus.

He pulls his woollen **tunic** more tightly around him.

His legs are bare and he has sandals on his feet. He is sitting on a horse at Hadrian's Wall in the far north of England. The wind whistles off the bare hills. It starts to rain.

Geordius is one of the soldiers guarding the long, high wall. It is taller than two adult men and stretches 118 kilometres (73 miles) from the west coast to the east coast of Britain. The Roman Emperor Hadrian built it to defend against raiders from the north.

It's a cold and lonely life. Geordius spends all day near one of the **milecastles** (each one is a mile apart along the wall).

"I ride along the top here and watch what people are doing down below. Usually they're just traders or farmers. Nothing much happens here."

LETTERS TO THE EDITOR

You tell Roman Britain what you think

SAY WHAT?

I come from Rome, and I like living in Britain. But one thing bothers me. Why don't the Brits speak properly? They jabber away in their funny languages and I can't understand a word. They should all speak Latin, like us.

Yours sincerely,

Sillius Twittus

Bristol, AD 150

SOFTY SOUTHERNERS

Central heating? Olive oil? Hot baths? Roast dormice? Figs? I reckon we're all going soft since the Romans arrived. When I was a young girl, we never had any of these luxuries. In fact, we had a cold bath every morning and porridge for every meal. Never did me any harm.

Yours sincerely,

Cassia Crosspatch (Mrs)

Inchtuthill, AD 225

WHY CAN'T I BE ROMAN?

The Emperor Caracalla has announced that everybody in the Empire is now a Roman citizen. Well, nearly everybody. Slaves don't count, of course. I'm a slave, so I'll never be a citizen and vote in elections or get all the rights that citizens have. It's a disgrace.

Yours sincerely,

Horatius Hackedoff

Chester, AD 212

CELEB NEWS

First with the latest about people who matter

CARATACUS
WOWS THE EMPEROR

By our Rome correspondent Gaius the Goss

Rome, AD 51

The great British leader Caratacus came to Rome as a villain. After years of fighting against the Roman invaders of Britain, he was captured at last. He was dragged to Rome in chains. Caratacus and his family were paraded in front of the jeering crowds. It seemed certain he would be put to death.

But Caratacus still wasn't beaten. After the parade, he came face to face with the mighty Emperor Claudius. Did he grovel, like the other captives? Not at all. Local reporter Cornelius Tacitus told me that Caratacus made a stirring speech. He demanded that Claudius set him free. The Emperor was so moved by these words that he ordered his guards to remove Caratacus's chains. His family was also released. Now the crowds cheered. The Briton wasn't a villain any more – he was a hero!

CELEB NEWS

DON'T MESS WITH THE EMPRESS

York, AD 210

Julia Domna is a tough egg. And she has to be. Her husband, the Emperor Septimius Severus, is old and ill. He has to be carried everywhere on a **litter**. Even so, he insists on leading his army against northern rebels. He has just got back from an expedition into Scotland.

Julia Domna went with him, staying in his military camp. She is a strong and intelligent woman. Septimius relies on her advice and respects her views. He has even had a special coin made that calls her "Mother of the Camp". Many people think she is the real power behind the throne.

WE'RE OFF TO SEE THE GIZZARD

AD 60

Meet Harry Spex. He's the hottest young **soothsayer** in Britain. This means he can see into the future. And how does he do that? Answer: by looking inside a chicken! By studying the livers and other bits, he can work out what the gods want us to do.

FASHION HIGHLIGHTS

STUBBLE AT THE DOUBLE

Special report by facial hair expert Mary Beard

Wroxeter, AD 120

Men! It's OK to grow a beard! For years, beards have been sneered at. People thought they were messy and dirty. But now our leader Hadrian has launched a whole new hairy trend. He's the first emperor ever to have a beard. Some say he grew it to hide scars on his face. Who cares? It looks great – so great, he's showing it off on his new coins.

FANCY FOOTWEAR

Our fashion editor, Vesta Pants, writes:

Wow! You'll just love poncing round town in these slinky new leather shoes. They're made of dark blue leather and are stitched with gold-coloured thread. Stunning!

SILVER SNAKES FROM SNETTISHAM

How about wrapping a snake round your wrist? Or slipping one on your finger? They're quite harmless – they're made of silver. Craftsmen here in East Anglia are making bracelets and rings in amazing new snake designs. With delicate patterns, they can even make the silver look like snakeskin. Snakes, of course, are popular in Rome because they are symbols of healing and rebirth.

Snettisham, Norfolk, AD 120

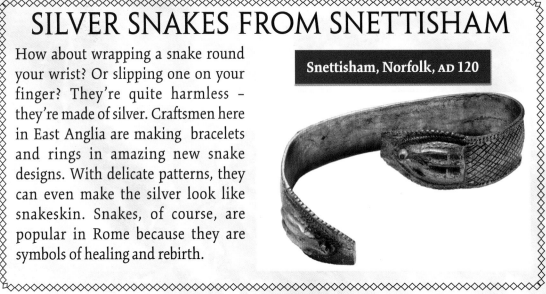

HANDY HINTS

Appius Larry answers your questions

Q

My next door neighbour has stolen one of my chickens. How do I put a curse on her?

A

Ask a god to help with your revenge. Get a thin sheet of lead and a stylus (pen), and write down what your neighbour has done. Then write down what horrible thing you want to happen to her. For a really strong curse, write it backwards. Leave the curse at the god's **sanctuary** *or chuck it in a spring (like the one at Bath).*

Q

I've been a slave all my life. How do I free myself?

A

You can buy your freedom, but you'll need to save money. This could take a long time, especially as a lot of slaves are paid very low wages - or nothing at all. If you're very lucky, your master might give you your freedom as a reward for loyal service.

Q

My girlfriend just told me I need a bath. I've never had one before. What shall I do about it?

A

It couldn't be easier. We Romans are crazy about washing. Some of us have a bath every day! Just go along to your local bathhouse and take off all your clothes (obviously). Start in the warm room (tepidarium), where you rub soap and oil into your body. Next comes the hot room (caldarium) - and that's really hot! You'll be glad to jump into the cold bath (frigidarium) at the end. You'll be a new man!

TRAVEL NEWS

HI TIDE!
Channel crossing terror

**By our seaside reporter
Rowena Boat**

Richborough, AD 45

We Romans aren't used to big rough seas. So the idea of crossing the Channel from Gaul to Britain scares us stiff. "Those waves are like mountains," said centurion Quintus Quivery, as he waited to board a ship for England. "I'm feeling seasick already."

Still, there are hundreds of soldiers making the journey. They are going to Britain to join the rest of the Roman army. The Romans have much of the island. Now we need to make our forces stronger to stay in control.

But there's another big problem. How do you make sure your boat gets safely over, without being blown miles off course?

I asked ship's captain Sergius Saltyface. He said:

"Very tricky. You have to leave Gaul when the tide's going out. That carries you to the middle of the Channel. Then you catch the tide that's going in to the English shore."

TRAVEL NEWS

GOING STRAIGHT

London, AD 180

We've nearly done it! The Roman network of roads across southern Britain is almost complete. There are hundreds of miles of them, joining up all the big towns and forts. Many of them run straight, and they're all topped with stones and gravel. No more mud and puddles.

Soldiers built them, and now soldiers can march along them at high speed to wherever they are needed. But many other people use the roads. Messengers gallop on horseback, carrying vital news. **Pedlars** and merchants carry their goods from town to town.

ON THE ROAD

Get out your chariot and go for a spin! Here are some favourite getaway routes:

- **Ermine Street** runs from London to York
- **Fosse Way** runs from Exeter to Lincoln
- **Icknield Street** runs from Stow-on-the-Wold to Rotherham
- **Stanegate** runs from Carlisle to Corbridge
- **Watling Street** runs from Richborough to Caerleon.

ROUND THE END OF BRITAIN

It's true – Britain really is an island! The great Roman general Agricola has proved this by sending ships to sail right round the north of Scotland.

HOMES FOR SALE

HALTWHISTLE, NORTHUMBERLAND

BARGAIN
OF THE WEEK

Fancy living on Hadrian's Wall? Here's your chance. This huge fort used to be full of soldiers. Now they've gone. It's just you and the sheep, so there's loads of room. There is a gatehouse and a **barrack block**, plus a swanky home where the commanding officer used to live! From the top of the **ramparts** you get amazing views of the River Tyne.

Price: 20 years' supply of barley beer

WROXETER, SHROPSHIRE

Enjoy the good life in this stunning country villa. It boasts a huge dining room decorated with painted frescoes on the walls, as well as a kitchen and bedrooms. There's even a porter's lodge. Features include central heating and a state-of-the-art bathhouse. Outside there are grand pillared walkways to front and rear, plus a beautiful sheltered courtyard. The owner wants a quick sale as he is going back to Rome.

Price: 10,000 gold bars

HOMES FOR SALE

LONDON

You'll get an amazing view of the city from this top-floor apartment. OK, so you have to climb three flights of stairs to get there AND these are the smallest flats in the whole insula (block). There's just one bedroom and one living room, and the flat has no heating or running water. But there's a fountain five minutes' walk away and you won't find anything cheaper in London.

Price: Two plucked chickens

BODRIFTY, CORNWALL

Wake up to the sound of waves crashing on the shore below. This old-fashioned Cornish roundhouse was once owned by Ancient Britons, but has been empty ever since AD 43. It's built to last. The walls are made of huge blocks of stone and the roof is made of timber and reeds. The doorway faces south-east – that's towards the morning sun and away from the Atlantic winds. It's handy for the Cornish tin mines too.

Price: A big pile of tin

FOOD AND DRINK

OO-ER – IT'S FOREIGN FOOD!

By our special guest, British Food Reporter, Gavo the Gannet

London, AD 50

We Brits are having to get used to eating strange new things. The Romans have been bringing over their favourite foods from Italy. There are figs and dates for a start. Yummy – but a bit odd-looking. There are grapes, and olive oil to make the food tastier, and wine to drink. They even eat snails!

Weirdest of all is the stuff Romans call garum. It is, basically, rotten fish guts. You take the insides from several fish and mix them with salt. Then you leave the mixture for a few months while it bubbles away. Strain off the liquid, and you've got garum. Romans love to spice up their food with it, but it still smells disgusting.

NEW VEG

The vegetable patch has certainly changed since the Romans came here. Here are some of the new vegetables, fruit, nuts and herbs you can grow:

leeks
asparagus
cabbage
carrots
celery
peas
turnips

mulberries

chestnuts
walnuts

rosemary
thyme

FOOD AND DRINK

STUFF YOUR FACE

OUR REGULAR REVIEW OF POSH EATERIES

This week: Great Witcombe,
by banquet correspondent Cora Napple

Gloucestershire, AD 120

What a feast! The grand dining hall here at Great Witcombe was the perfect setting for an amazing meal. The men and women lay on couches, leaning on their left elbows and eating with their right hands.

The banquet started with wine mixed with honey. There were pieces of delicious sugary bread to dip into it. Then came the main course. Wow! I've never seen so much meat. The table was packed with wild boar, venison, goose, chicken and hare, all perfectly cooked. And after that was the dessert of apples and other fruit.

I couldn't eat another thing. But we weren't finished yet. Slaves carried in huge dishes of eels, oysters and other shellfish. No wonder so many of the diners soon fell fast asleep.

ARTS AND ENTERTAINMENT

MOSAIC MAGIC

DISH OF THE GODS

London, AD 190

Today a stunning new masterpiece was unveiled. Crowds gathered to get their first glimpse of London's latest floor mosaic. It shows the Roman god **Bacchus**. He holds a **staff** and cup, and wears a laurel wreath on his head.

Bacchus is also riding on the back of a tiger. The tiger is holding up a paw, as if she is moving.

"Blimey! That tiger's very lifelike", said local housewife, Didia Seethat. "You wouldn't get me up on one of those things."

The mosaic is made of hundreds of tiny pieces of stone, tile and glass. They come in all sorts of glowing colours – black, grey, white, red, pink and turquoise. The pieces are stuck onto a bed of cement. Sounds easy, doesn't it? But it takes a lot of skill and training.

The **silversmiths** of Suffolk have come up with something special. The Great Dish of Mildenhall is one of the great treasures of Roman Britain. Made of pure silver, its beautiful design shows gods and heroes, including **Oceanus**, **Hercules** and Bacchus. Go and see it if you can.

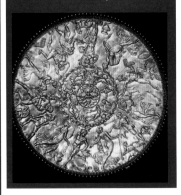

GET YOUR COPIES OF
THE GOLDEN ASS

A HILARIOUS NEW BESTSELLER BY LUCIUS APULEIUS

Read about the boy who plays with magic – and is turned into a donkey!

BONA BOOKS LTD, LONDON

ARTS AND ENTERTAINMENT

Thundering Hooves

Ribchester, AD 190

It's the nearest thing to a battle – and almost as dangerous! The Ribchester **cavalry** held their annual games yesterday, and it was a terrifying experience. The Hippika Gymnasia, as it's called, is a breathtaking display of skill by these brave horse soldiers.

Two teams of cavalrymen rode out in tight formation. One team suddenly turned and galloped at the other, throwing **javelins** and trying to knock them out of their saddles. The other team attacked in turn. Next, the two teams rode in opposite circles, still throwing javelins. The final two events featured more amazing battle skills. The soldiers showed how they could turn in the saddle and defend themselves against an enemy behind them.

The display closed with men in full armour jumping onto their horses – when they're galloping at top speed! No wonder our enemies are so scared of the Roman cavalry.

FOR SALE

HOUSEHOLD

Pair of child's sandals

Genuine leather, with **hobnails** on the sole. Will never wear out.

Household god

Small stone figure of the goddess Venus, for use in your home **shrine**. Slight damage: right arm missing.

Woman's tunic

Brand new ankle-length garment, woven from pure cotton. Plus woollen **stola** to wear over it and keep you warm this winter.

Bronze helmet

As worn by legionaries. Cheek protectors and plume included. Worn once. Big dent on right-hand side.

Strigil

Every bather needs one. Scrape off that soap 'n' sweat at the bathhouse with this classic metal **strigil**. Unwanted present.

FARM AND GARDEN

Snail sale

5,000 Roman snails, raised on the farm. Low price for quick deal. Ideal starter for your next banquet. Owner leaving the country.

Iron sickle

The perfect tool for cutting wheat and barley. Well looked after, with sharp blade and comfy wooden handle.

Cartload of carrots

The Romans' favourite! Grown too many this year so selling on. Could be fed to cavalry horses.

SERVICES

Learn Latin

Hobnob with the cream of society in their own language! Our two-day course will teach you the basics of Latin, as spoken in Rome. Contact Latin IV U.

Evil Eye

Do you want revenge? Got a grudge against someone? Call us at Curse First Ltd – we curse first, we curse best!

Amphorae

We buy and sell second-hand storage jars. Guaranteed solid Roman pottery, suitable for wine or olive oil. *For the best prices come to Amphora Penny.*

JOBS

Mosaic sorter

Wanted: young person to sort piles of stone and glass pieces by colour and shape. Must have tough hands.

Glass blower

Got a lot of puff? Then you're just the one we need to blow into molten glass to make jugs and goblets. Apply to Class Glass, Glasgow.

Join the army

Become a Roman legionary today. Learn to use weapons and bash people about. See the world – the Empire stretches all the way to Egypt and the Black Sea!

Fishwife

Oh, my cod! There's a vacancy at our local fish market – now fill-et! Women wanted to clean fish six hours a day. Bring your own soap.

TIMELINE

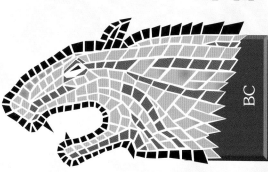

BC

55 BC
Julius Caesar fails in first attempt to invade Britain

54 BC
Julius Caesar fails in second attempt to invade Britain

AD

AD 43
Claudius invades Britain. British forces surrender at Colchester.

C. AD 50
London becomes an important trading centre after a bridge is built across the Thames

AD 51
British leader Caratacus captured and taken to Rome. Later pardoned and released.

AD 60
Iceni Queen Boudicca leads revolt against Romans, destroying Colchester and London

AD 82
Ships sent by Agricola sail around north coast of Scotland

C. AD 90
Work begins on baths and temple complex at Bath

C. AD 110
Gold mining in full swing at Dolaucothi, Wales

C. AD 120
Hadrian visits Britain. Work begins on Hadrian's Wall.

C. AD 180
Basic network of Roman roads in Britain complete

C. AD 190
Bacchus mosaic completed in London

AD 210
Septimius Severus campaigns against rebels in Scotland

C. AD 250
Alban put to death for being a Christian

AD 287
Roman coins minted in London for the first time

AD 312
Emperor Constantine allows freedom of worship for Christians

C. AD 340
Chedworth Villa extended

AD 410
Last Roman troops leave Britain

GLOSSARY

amber yellow or brown hardened tree sap used to make jewellery

amphitheatre oval or round space with seats, used for sport and other contests

Bacchus Roman god of wine

Baltic area of land near the Baltic Sea, in the eastern Atlantic Ocean

barrack block block of buildings that soldiers live in

cargo goods carried by ship

cavalry soldiers on horses

Channel (English) piece of sea that divides Britain from mainland Europe

Druid priest, magician or soothsayer from ancient times

forge place where blacksmiths make or shape metal objects by heating them in a fire or furnace

forum public square or marketplace used in Roman times to discuss business or law

Gaul ancient region of Europe. The area covers modern-day France, Belgium, south-west Germany, the southern Netherlands and north Italy.

Hercules famous and very strong hero from Greek legend

hobnail short nail with a thick head, used to protect the bottoms of shoes

household gods images of gods kept in small shrines in people's homes

Iceni tribe of ancient Britons who lived in an area of south-eastern England

javelin long spear made for throwing

legionary Roman soldier

litter sort of bed in the form of a carriage, in which rich people were carried around by slaves

milecastles small forts that housed Roman soldiers along Hadrian's Wall

mint place where coins are made

mosaic picture or pattern made with small pieces of stone or glass

nymph female nature spirit, often connected with natural features such as springs or streams

Oceanus god of the sea in Greek and Roman legend

pedlar traveller who goes around the country selling goods

ramparts space on the top of a wall in a fort, where soldiers kept watch

revolt violent action against a ruler or government

sanctuary holy place such as a temple, shrine or church

shears tool-like scissors used for cutting the wool from sheep

shrine holy site where people worship

sickle short-handled farming tool with a blade in the shape of a semi-circle

silversmith person who makes things from silver

soothsayer person who claims to be able to see into the future

staff long stick

stola woman's version of a toga

strigil metal tool used for scraping the skin after a bath

temple place dedicated to the worship of a god

tide twice-daily rise and fall of the oceans due to the pull of the Moon. The Romans came from the Mediterranean Sea, where there is no tide.

tribe group of people who claim to have the same ancestors

tunic loose-fitting garment reaching as far as the knees

venison meat from a wild deer

FIND OUT MORE

There's a lot more to discover about the Romans in Britain. And new discoveries are being made all the time. Read about them in books or online, or visit some of the hundreds of forts, villas, bathhouses and other great sites from the period. Here's just a tiny selection to get you started.

BOOKS

100 Facts: Roman Britain, Philip Steele (Miles Kelly, 2015)

Life in Roman Britain, Anita Ganeri (Raintree, 2015)

Roman Britain, Izzi Howell (Wayland, 2016)

Roman Britain (Found), Moira Butterfield (Franklin Watts, 2017)

Roman Britain (The History Detective Investigates), Peter Hepplewhite (Wayland 2014)

WEBSITES

www.bbc.co.uk/guides/z9j4kqt

Discover more about how the Romans conquered Britain.

http://www.britishmuseum.org/learning/schools_and_teachers/resources/cultures/ancient_rome.aspx

This British Museum site uses real Roman remains and treasures to explore what really happened in Roman Britain.

http://www.primaryhomeworkhelp.co.uk/Romans.html

This site gives basic facts about many aspects of Roman Britain.

PLACES TO VISIT

Britain is covered with Roman remains of all sorts. Most can be visited or seen in museums. Is there something near you?

The British Museum
Great Russell Street
London WC1B 3DG

A huge collection of many wonderful things, including mosaics and the Mildenhall Dish.

Chedworth Roman Villa
Chedworth, Chletenham, Gloucestershire
GL54 3LJ

One of the largest villas of Roman Britain.

Dolaucothi Gold Mine
Pumsaint, Llanwrda, Carmarthenshire
SA19 8US

Take a tour of a Roman gold mine.

Hadrian's Wall Path
Wallsend, Tyne and Wear, to Bowness-on-Solway, Cumbria

Much of the Wall still remains – about 135 kilometres (84 miles) of it. There are forts, museums and many other great sites to see.

Museum of London
150 London Wall, London EC2Y 5HN

Thousands of enthralling exhibits.

The Roman Baths
Stall Street, Bath, BA1 1LZ

The most famous Roman site in Britain.

Vindolanda
Bardon Mill, Hexham, Northumberland
NE4 7JN

Exciting excavation of a Roman fort – and there's the Roman Army Museum too!

INDEX

Alban 9
arts and entertainment 26–27
Aulus Plautius 6

baths, Roman 10, 12, 15, 19, 22, 28
Boudicca, Queen 7
Britons 4, 5, 6, 7, 9, 16, 23, 24
business 10–11

Caratacus 16
Chedworth Roman villa 12
Claudius, Emperor 4, 6, 16
clothing 18, 28
coins, Roman 11, 18
Colchester 4, 6, 7
Constantine, Emperor 9

Dolaucothi gold mines 11
Druids 8

English Channel 5, 20

farming 12–13, 28
fashion 18
food and drink 5, 13, 24–25, 28
for sale, items 28

Gaul 5 10, 20
gods 8, 9, 17, 26
gold 11, 22
Great Witcombe 25

Hadrian, Emperor 14, 18
Hadrian's Wall 14 22
handy hints 19
Hippika Gymnasia 27
homes 4, 12, 22–23, 28
horses 14, 21 27 28

Iceni tribe 7
invasion 4, 5, 6, 7, 16, 20

Julia Domna 17
Julius Caesar 5, 6

language 15, 28
Latin 4, 15, 28
Letters to the Editor 15
London 4, 7, 10, 11, 21, 23, 24, 26

Mildenhall Dish 26
mosaic 12, 26, 28

religion 8–9
Ribchester cavalry 27
roads, Roman 4, 21
Roman Empire 4, 6, 10, 15, 28
Rome 5, 6, 8, 9, 15, 16, 28

Scotland 17, 21
ships 5, 10, 20, 21
slavery 11, 15, 16, 19, 25
Snettisham bracelet 18
soldiers, Roman 6, 7, 9, 13, 14, 20, 21,
    22, 27
soothsayers 17
Suetonius Paullinus 7

Thames, River 5, 6, 10
trade 10, 14
travel 20–21

villas *see* homes